Revolution and Romanticism, 1789-1834
A series of facsimile reprints chosen and introduced by
Jonathan Wordsworth

Bürger
Leonora 1796

Gottfried Augustus Bürger

Leonora

1796

translated by J. T. Stanley

Woodstock Books
Otley · Washington D.C.
2000

This edition first published 2000 by
Woodstock Books
Otley, West Yorkshire
England LS21 3JP
and
Books International
PO Box 605, Herndon
VA 20172, U.S.A.

ISBN 1 85477 232 5
Reproduced by permission from a copy in
The Bodleian Library, University of Oxford,
shelfmark Vet. Δ 673
Introduction copyright © 2000 Jonathan Wordsworth

British Library Cataloguing-in-Publication Data
A catalogue record for this book is
available from the British Library

Library of Congress Cataloging-in-Publication Data
applied for

Printed and bound in England by
Smith Settle
Otley LS21 3JP

Introduction

Looking back in his *Historic Survey of German Poetry*, William Taylor (never named without his sobriquet, 'of Norwich') claimed to have eight different English versions of *Lenore* lying on his table, and to have read still more. He himself had created the vogue for Bürger's ballad, translating it in 1790, and prompting imitation by distributing it among friends, not all of whom kept the poem to themselves. Some of the copies he possessed, or had read in a lifetime devoted to German poetry, may have been in manuscript, but five printed versions belong to the single year, 1796: his own *Lenora: A Ballad from Bürger*, held back for five years, then published in the Original Poetry section of the *Monthly Magazine* for March '96; *William and Helen*, published anonymously by the young Walter Scott, who had heard Taylor's poem read in Edinburgh in 1794 (and made his own translation before any rival appeared in print); *Leonora, A Tale*, translated by J.T.Stanley F.R.S, with Blake frontis-, head- and tail-pieces (preface dated 15 April, first edition anonymous); *Ellenore, A Ballad*, translated by the Poet Laureate, Henry James Pye (published before Stanley, though written later); and *Leonora*, translated by W.R.Spencer, with frontispiece and full-page illustrations by Lady Diana Beauclerk.

Gottfried Augustus Bürger had written *Lenore* twenty-five years before its publication in England, along with *Des Pfarrers Tochter von Taubenhain* (translated by Taylor as *The Lass of Fair Wone*, source of Wordsworth's *Thorn*), and *Der Wilde Jaeger* (translated by Scott as *The Chase*, source of Wordsworth's *Hart-Leap Well*). British audiences had not at once been ready for Bürger's *sturm und drang*, and there had been no early translations. The ballad's impact in Germany, however, like that of Schiller's *Die Räuber* (first performance 1781, translated 1792), had been immediate. Commenting more generally on Bürger's strengths, Taylor offers a vignette of the poet's first reading of his ballad to the literary circle of Göttingen:

His extraordinary powers of language are founded on a rejection of the conventional phraseology of regular poetry, in favour of popular forms of expression, caught by the listening artist from the voice of agitated nature. Imitative harmony he pursues almost to excess: the *onomatopoeia* is his prevailing figure; the interjection his favourite part of speech: arrangement, rhythm, sound, rhyme, are always with him an echo of the sense ... The effect was particularly great on the younger Count Stolberg. During the stanza,

> Anon an iron-grated door
> Fast biggens on their view;
> He cracks his whip – the locks, the bolts,
> Cling clang! asunder flew ...

Frederick Leopold started from his seat in an agony of rapturous terror.

(*Historic Survey* ii ,20-1)

Driven to blasphemy by grief at the failure of her soldier to return from the war, Lenore wishes herself dead. Wilhelm appears to claim his bride, and together they gallop through the night on his preternatural war-horse to the grave that is their wedding-bed. Count Stolberg's 'rapturous terror' seems extreme. But there is no reason to think it ungenuine, or even exaggerated. Taken with the burst of English translations in 1796 (the year of Lewis's *Monk*, two years after Radcliffe's *Mysteries of Udolpho*), it requires from us an uncondescending response to the gothic. We are (if at all possible) to be shocked by the iron-grated door that 'biggens' to our view, letting us into the purlieus of Death. Taylor has not made the task simpler by quoting Bürger in the pseudo-medieval lines of his own translation. But the original is not that much easier to take seriously –

> Rasch auf ein eisern Gitterthor
> Ging's mit verhängtem Zügel;
> Mit schwanker Gert' ein Schlag davor,
> Zersprengte Schloss und Riegel.   (st. 29, 1-4)

– and Taylor's competitors, though their diction may be less extravagant, are none of them very convincing. Scott reduces the passage to two inconsequential lines,

> Reluctant on its rusty hinge
> Revolved an iron door ...   (st.59, 1-2)

that leave the door ungrated and unexplained, and exclude the horse's impressive violence, as he bursts through bolt and bar ('Zersprengte Schloss und Riegel'). Stanley is uninspired, offering little more than paraphrase:

> High grated iron doors, in vain
> Barr'd their way. With loosened rein
>   Whilst William urg'd the steed,
> He struck the bolts – they open flew ...   (st. 32, 1-4)

Pye, though claiming to be more accurate, inserts a final line solely for the rhyme:

> 'Gainst an iron-grated door
>   Fierce with loosened rein he drives;
> The ponderous bars resist no more,
>   Even a touch their hinges rives.   (st.29, 1-4)

It may be that Spencer, though scarcely closer to Bürger's wording, is closer to his spirit:

> Full at a portal's massy gate
> The plunging steed impetuous dash'd:
> At the dread shock, wall, bars, and gate,
> Hurl'd down with headlong ruin crash'd.

Bürger's idiom is extremely difficult to copy. On second thoughts, Taylor's dating of his ballad back to the Crusades, and, with it, the decision to use a pseudo-medieval diction (closer far to Chatterton than Chaucer), come to seem inspired. Medievalism, skin-deep though it is, works for *Lenora* as it will work for *The Ancyente Marinere* (Coleridge's tribute to Bürger), by enhancing the otherness of a supernatural narrative, at the same time making both superstition and moral crudity more easily acceptable. Taylor is enabled positively to heighten improbability in *Lenora*, having his spectral steed (in a passage preferred by Wordsworth to the original) cross sea as well as land:

> The bridges thunder as they pass,
>> But earthlie soune is none.
>
> Tramp, tramp, across the land they speede;
>> Splash, splash, across the see:
> 'Hurrah! the dead can ride apace;
>> Dost feare to ride with mee?'

Bürger is nowhere more impressive in his repetition and onomatopoeia. Taylor, whose commentary in the *Historic Survey* is much of it repeated from his 1796 introduction to Bürger in the *Monthly*, is to be seen in his translation rejecting 'conventional phraseology ... in favour of popular forms of expression, caught by the listening artist from the voice of agitated nature'. He could hardly have forecast the publication two years later of *Lyrical Ballads*, or the part his Bürger-translations would have in the ushering in of a new poetry, but it is most obviously through him that Bürger has his place in English literary history.

Other translators of 1796, however, have an importance that has not been recognized. Spencer places Bürger squarely in a gothic tradition by reference in his Preface to 'the impregnable towers of Otranto'. *Lenore*, for him, is the most perfect German production of the kind initiated by Walpole. Its story 'in a narrow compass unites tragic event, poetical surprise, and epic regularity'. To what purpose? Not pleasure (as we might suppose) in gothic extravagance, but as an instance of sublime retribution. The despair of Lenore is 'at once natural and criminal' – words are being carefully chosen – her punishment is 'dreadful, but equitable'. 'Few objections', Spencer continues, 'can be made to a subject, new, simple, and striking; and none to a moral, which cannot be to frequently or too awfully enforced'. If we turn, in Spencer's version, to the moral to which no objection can be made, it is to be reminded that fiends in Bürger howl the judgment of God:

> Throng'd in the moon's eclipsing shade,
> Of fiends and shapes a spectre crowd
> Dance featly round th' expiring maid,
> And howl this awful lesson loud:
> 'Learn patience, though thy heart should break,
> Nor seek God's mandates to controul!
> Now this cold earth thy dust shall take,
> And Heaven relenting take thy soul!'

So strict are the 'mandates' that only a divine relenting, a going-back on God's intention to damn eternally, can rescue one who has dared –

> Thus did the demons of despair
> Her wildered sense to madness strain   (st. 12, 1-2)

– to say that the return of her lover is more important to her than the fate of her soul.

It is Stanley, among the translators, who takes the extreme step of rewriting Bürger's text. 'Since the first publication of this poem', he writes in the Advertisement,

I have often doubted whether it was not calculated ... to injure the cause of Religion and Morality, by exhibiting a representation of supernatural interference, inconsistent to our ideas of a just and benevolent Deity.

It is of more importance than is generally believed, both to human happiness and virtue, that the Being we adore should be considered as amiable and impartial, and not as either capricious or morose.

The tones are earnest in the extreme. Whatever the motives of his fellow-translators (Taylor fascinated by German literary achievement; Scott, dazzled by the possibilities of a ballad-form, up-to-date and unnostalgic; Pye congratulating himself as Laureate on being more accurate), Stanley is striving to do the right thing. And striving against the gothic – 'those who think the merit of the poem consists in its power of exciting terror'. 'What opinion', he asks (as we have to ask, if we seek to know the impact of *Lenore* in its earliest English context),

of either the kindness, or the justice of Providence, can be formed from the description of a young girl exposed to the most cruel of all punishments, abandoned to the malignity of every fiend of Hell let loose for her destruction, only because in the first paroxysms of despair and agony, for the supposed loss of a lover, thinking God indifferent about her fate, she refused all comfort, and wished for death?

The fiends of Hell are believed in. So is destruction of the soul. Perhaps too, the terrible possibility of an indifferent God.

In the circumstances Stanley contrives a final section in the manner of *Faust*, and of Bürger's *Wilde Jaeger*, in which forces, bad and good, contend for Leonora's soul, and (uniquely) it is the good that wins:

> Wild, snorting fire, the courser rear'd,
> As wrapp'd in smoke he disappear'd,
>   Poor Leonora fell;
> The hideous spectres hover round,
> Deep groans she heard from under ground,
>   And fiends ascend from hell.　(st. 35)

The writing becomes markedly stronger as the labours of translation give way to new creation:

> They dance and cry, in dreadful howl,
> 'She asks no mercy for her soul;
>   Her earthly course is done.
> When mortals, rash and impious! dare
> Contend with God, and court despair,
>   We claim them as our own.'

> 'Yet', thus was heard, in milder strains,
> 'Call on the Lord, while life remains,
>   Unite your heart to his;
> When Man repents, and is resign'd,
> God loves to soothe his suff'ring mind,
>   And grant him future bliss.'　(sts 36-37)

It is, of course, what Stanley wishes to believe. But it is also Christian doctrine. Bürger, whether carried beyond his beliefs by the gothic impulse, or personally conceiving of a retributive God, has created a morality that must be

shocking to the ordinary believer. Stanley returns his readers
to the God of love:

> Leonora, e'er her sense was gone,
> Thus faint exclaim'd – 'thy Will be done,
>   Lord let thy anger cease.'
> Soft on the wind was borne the pray'r;
> The spectres vanish'd into air,
>   And all was hush'd in peace. (st. 39)

All seems to be concluded. We have an ending that would
have done its job admirably. But Stanley, in a way that
couldn't be simpler, or (on the level of this more-or-less
allegorical narrative) more satisfying, intervenes to fulfill
hopes that have never been permitted. Leonora awakes.
William returns. If Taylor created the vogue for Bürger,
finding too the closest approximation to the excitement of
his style, Stanley has arrived at a meaningful rewriting and
rethinking that permits the story of *Lenore* to be read on the
level not merely of the gothic, but of his readers' personal
faith.

J.W.

Blake inv:

Perry. sc:

O! how I dreamt of things impossible.
Of Death affecting Forms least like himself;
I've seen, or dreamt I saw the Tyrant dress,
Lay by his Horrors, and put on his Smiles;

Treacherous he came an unexpected Guest,
Nay, though invited by the loudest Calls
Of blind Imprudence, unexpected still;
And then, he dropt his Mask.

Alter'd from Young.

L E O N O R A.

A TALE,

TRANSLATED AND ALTERED FROM THE

𝔊𝔈𝔯𝔪𝔞𝔫

OF

GOTTFRIED AUGUSTUS BŰRGER.

~~~~~~

BY J. T. STANLEY, ESQ. F. R. S. &c.

═══

" Poetry hath Bubbles, as the water has :
" And thefe are of them."——

~~~~~~

Does not th' idea of a God include
The notion of beneficent and good ;
Of one to mercy, not revenge inclin'd,
Able and willing to relieve mankind ?

═══

A NEW EDITION.

~~~~~~

LONDON:
PRINTED BY S. GOSNELL,
FOR WILLIAM MILLER, OLD BOND STREET.

~~~~

1796.

ADVERTISEMENT

TO THE

PRESENT EDITION.

~~~~~

THE favourable manner in which the tranflation of "Leonora," offered by me to the Public, has been received, I feel highly flattering, as a proof, my opinion of the work was not erroneous, when I thought it worthy being fubmitted to their perufal.

When the laft Edition was nearly exhaufted, I intimated to Mr. Stanley, (whom now I am allowed to name as the Tranf-lator of the poem,) my intention to re-publifh it on a larger fized paper, accompanied by fome new Engravings; he, in con-fequence, was pleafed to fend me, after an interval of fome days, a

b   copy

copy of his Tranflation, much altered, and much enlarged, together with a letter, which, having his permiffion, as it ftates his
reafons for deviating from the ftory originally related by Burger,
I fhall here infert.

" Dear Sir,

    " I HAVE fent you, according to my
" promife, a corrected copy of the tranflation of Burger's Leonora.
" Tranflation, indeed, I ought fcarcely now to call it; for I have
" fo altered and added to the original, that the ftory in its Englifh
" drefs, has acquired a character, altogether new and peculiarly
" its own.

" Since your firft publication of the poem, I have often doubted
" whether it was not calculated (as far as its effects could extend)
" to injure the caufe of Religion and Morality, by exhibiting
" a reprefentation of fupernatural interference, inconfiftent with
" our ideas of a juft and benevolent Deity.

" It is of more importance than is generally believed, both to
" human happinefs and virtue, that the Being we adore fhould be
            " confidered

" considered as amiable and impartial, and not as either capricious
" or morofe. Obedience to his will fhould furely be procured
" from men (if poffible) by an appeal, rather to their affections,
" than to their fears; but what opinion of either the kindnefs,
" or juftice of Providence, can be formed from the defcription of a
" young girl expofed to the moft cruel of all punifhments,
" abandoned to the malignity of every fiend of Hell let loofe
" for her deftruction, only becaufe in the firft paroxyfms of defpair
" and agony, for the fuppofed lofs of a lover, thinking God
" indifferent about her fate, fhe refufed all comfort, and wifhed
" for death.

" Such reflections have tempted me to make the alterations I
" have alluded to. I am, however, doubtful whether they will
" be approved of by the public. Thofe who think the merit of
" the Poem confifts in its power of exciting terror, and who love
" to retain the impreffion of fuch fentiments when once excited, will
" probably condemn every deviation from the original, as preju-
" dicial to its interefts; but, on the other hand, many may pre-
" fer it, as it will appear in your new Edition, who think
" that the firft object of all writing, particularly of all poetry, as
" bearing

" bearing the character of more studied composition, should be
" to teach men clear ideas of justice and injustice, vice and
" virtue.—They will be pleased to find the Almighty no longer
" held out to their contemplation as an irritable and vindictive
" ruler, ever watchful for offence, and prepared to punish ; but in-
" stead, as the friend and affectionate parent, having but one interest
" with his creatures, happy in their happiness, and associated to
" their nature in the captivating forms of sympathy and love.

" I am, dear Sir, truly your's,

" *Bolton-Row, April 15, 1796.*"   " I. T. S."

The Public will judge between the merits of the first, and this
new publication of Leonora, and it remains with me only to ex-
press my hopes that no purchaser of the former edition will be dif-
pleased at the appearance of another so much altered, and to inform
such as may be desirous of exchanging the one for the other, that
I shall, at all times, be ready to obey their orders.

Old Bond-Street.   W. M.

PREFACE.

PREFACE.

~~~~~~

THE following little Poem was tranſlated by a reſpectable friend of the publiſher, who, being favoured with a peruſal, was much pleaſed with its wild originality; and he has thought himſelf fortunate in obtaining permiſſion to lay it before the public.

The German author, conſcious, perhaps, of the latitude he gives his imagination, was willing to ſhield himſelf under that liberty which poets are allowed the privilege of poſſeſſing: for the parody of the words

> " The earth hath bubbles, as the water has;
>
> " And theſe are of them"——

which are placed as a motto to the title-page, is to be found in a preface to a collection of his works, publiſhed by him in his own

C   country:

country :—And were it not for thefe *bubbles*, which nature, in her lavifh mode, fometimes permits to iffue from the mind, poetry would be deprived of many of her moft beautiful productions.

The Poem will be found, in many refpects, to have been altered from the original; but more particularly towards the conclufion, where the tranflator thinking the moral not fufficiently explained, has added feveral lines. The German poem concludes with a ftanza, the literal meaning of which may be given in the following words:

Now in the moonfhine, round and round,
    Link'd hand in hand, the fpirits fly;
And as they dance, in howling found,
    Have patience! patience! loud they cry.
    And ne'er with God in Heaven contend:
Though rack'd with forrow, be refign'd,
    Thy earthly courfe is at an end,
May God unto thy Soul be kind.

But in order to fhew more clearly what have been the variations and additions, a few copies of the German text will be printed,

which

which may be had, fewed up with the tranflation, by fuch as fhould be defirous of comparing the one with the other.

The fuccefs of fome late publications has proved that the wild and eccentric writings of the Germans are perufed with pleafure by the Englifh reader. " Leonora" is certainly not void of that fire and energy for which their authors are celebrated: It is therefore fubmitted to the perufal of the public, with the hope that it will not be lefs favourably received.

W. M.

Old Bond-Street, Feb. 8, 1786.

L E O N O R A.

~~~~~~

" Ah, William! art thou falſe or dead ?"
Cried Leonora from her bed.

  " I dreamt thou'dſt ne'er return."
William had fought in Frederick's hoſt
At Prague, but what his fate——if loſt
  Or ſafe, ſhe could not learn.

     B   Hungaria's

Hungaria's Queen, and Pruſſia's King,
Wearied, at length, with bickering,
 Reſolv'd to end the ſtrife ;
And homewards, then, their ſeparate routs
The armies took, with ſongs and ſhouts,
 With cymbals, drum, and fife.

As deck'd with boughs they march'd along,
From ev'ry door, the old and young
 Ruſh'd forth the troops to greet.
" Thank God," each child and parent cry'd,
And " welcome, welcome," many a bride,
 As friends long parted meet.

They joy'd, poor Leonora griev'd :
No kiſs ſhe gave, no kiſs receiv'd ;
 Of William none could tell ;
She wrung her hands, and tore her hair ;
Till left alone, in deep deſpair,
 Bereft of ſenſe ſhe fell.

         Swift

Swift to her aid, her mother came,

" Ah ! fay," fhe cried, " in mercy's name,

 " What means this frantic grief ?"

" Mother, 'tis paft—all hopes are fled,

" God hath no mercy, William's dead,

 " My woe is paft relief."

" Pardon, O pardon, Lord above !

" My child, with pray'rs invoke his love,

 " The Almighty never errs ;"

" O, mother ! mother ! idle prate,

" Can he be anxious for my fate,

 " Who never heard my prayers ?"

" Be patient, child, in God believe,

" The good he can, and will relieve,

 " To truft his power endeavour."

" O, mother ! mother ! all is vain,

" What truft can bring to life again ?

 " The paft, is paft, for ever.

" Who

" Who knows, but that he yet furvives ;

" Perchance, far off from hence he lives,

" And thinks no more of you.

" Forget, forget, the faithlefs youth,

" Away with grief, your forrow foothe,

" Since William proves untrue."

" Mother, all hope has fled my mind,

" The paft, is paft, our God's unkind ;

" Why did he give me breath ?

" Oh ! that this hated loathfome light

" Would fade for ever from my fight,

" Come, death, come, welcome death !"

" Indulgent Father, fpare my child,

" Her agony hath made her wild,

" She knows not what fhe does.

" Daughter, forget thy earthly love,

" Look up to him who reigns above,

" Where joys fucceed to woes."

" Mother,

" Mother, what now are joys to me ?

" With William, Hell a Heaven could be,

    " Without him, Heaven a Hell.

" Fade, fade away, thou hated light,

" Death, bear me hence to endleſs night,

    " With love all hope farewell."

Thus raſhly, Leonora ſtrove

To doubt the truth of heavenly love.

    She wept, and beat her breaſt ;

She pray'd for death, until the moon

With all the ſtars in ſilence ſhone,

    And ſooth'd the world to reſt.

When, hark ! without, what ſudden ſound !

She hears a trampling o'er the ground,

    Some horſeman muſt be near !

He ſtops, he rings. Hark ! as the noiſe

Dies ſoft away, a well-known voice

    Thus greets her liſt'ning ear.

          C   " Wake,

" Wake, Leonora ;—doſt thou ſleep,

" Or thoughtleſs laugh, or conſtant weep,

    " Is William welcome home ?"

" Dear William, you !—return'd, and well !

" I've wak'd and wept—but why, ah ! tell,

    " So late—at night you come ?"

" At midnight only dare we roam,

" For thee from Prague, though late, I come."

    " For me !—ſtay here and reſt ;

" The wild winds whiſtle o'er the waſte,

" Ah, deareſt William ! why ſuch haſte ?

    " Firſt warm thee in my breaſt."

" Let the winds whiſtle o'er the waſte,

" My duty bids me be in haſte ;

    " Quick, mount upon my ſteed :

" Let the winds whiſtle far and wide,

" Ere morn, two hundred leagues we'll ride,

    " To reach our marriage bed."

                         " What,

" What, William! for a bridal room,

" Travel to night fo far from home ?"

    " Leonora, 'tis decreed.

" Look round thee, love, the moon fhines clear,

" The dead ride fwiftly; never fear,

    " We'll reach our marriage bed."

" Ah, William! whither would'ft thou fpeed,

" What! where! this diftant marriage bed ?"

    " Leonora, no delay.

" 'Tis far from hence; ftill—cold—and fmall :

" Six planks, no more, compofe it all ;

    " Our guefts await, away !"

She lightly on the courfer fprung,

And her white arms round William flung,

    Like to a lily wreath.

In fwifteft gallop off they go,

The ftones and fparks around they throw,

    And pant the way for breath.

                         The

The objects fly on every fide,
The bridges thunder as they ride;
   " Art thou my love afraid?
" Death fwiftly rides, the moon fhines clear,
" The dead doth Leonora fear?"
   " Ah, no!—why name the dead?"

Hark! as their rapid courfe they urge,
A paffing bell, and folemn dirge;
   Hoarfe ravens join the ftrain.
They fee a coffin on a bier,
A prieft and mourners too appear,
   Slow moving o'er the plain.

And fad was heard the funeral lay;
" What the Lord gives, he takes away;
   " Life's but a fleeting fhade.
" A tale that's told,—a flower that falls;
" Death, when the leaft expected, calls,
   " And bears us to his bed."

Forbear,

" Forbear ;"—imperious William cry'd,

" I carry home, a beauteous bride,

 " Come, to our marriage feaft ;

" Mourners, away, we want your fong ;

" And as we fwiftly hafte along,

 " Give us your bleffing, prieft.

" Sing on, that life is like a fhade,

" A tale that's told, or flowers which fade ;

 " Such ftrains will yield delight.

" And, when we to our chamber go,

" Bury your dead, with wail and woe ;

 " The fervice fuits the night."

While William fpeaks, they filent ftand,

Then run obedient to command.

 But, on with furious bound,

The foaming courfer forward flew,

Fire and ftones his heels purfue,

 Like whirlwinds dafh'd around.

D   **On**

On right and left, on left and right,
Trees, hills, and towns flew paſt their ſight,
    As on they breathleſs preſt ;
" With the bright moon, like death we ſpeed,
" Doth Leonora fear the dead ?"
     " Ah ! leave the dead at reſt."

Behold, where in the moon's pale beam,
As wheels and gibbets faintly gleam,
    Join'd hand in hand, a crowd
Of imps and ſpeſtres hover nigh,
Or round a waſted wretch they fly,
    When William calls aloud :

" Hither, ye airy rabble, come,
" And follow till I reach my home ;
    " We want a marriage dance."
As when the leaves on wither'd trees,
Are ruſtled by an eddying breeze,
    The muttering ſprites advance.

                                  But,

But, foon with hurried fteps, the crew
Rufh'd prattling on, for William flew,
 Clafp'd by the frighted fair:
Swifter than fhafts, or than the wind,
While ftruck from earth, fire flafh'd behind,
 Like lightnings through the air.

Not only flew the landfcape by,
The clouds and ftars appear'd to fly.
 " Thus over hills and heath
" We ride like death ; fay, lovely maid,
" By moon-light doft thou fear the dead?"
 " Ah! fpeak no more of death."

" The cock hath crow'd.—Away! away!
" The fand ebbs out: I fcent the day.
 " On! on! away from here!
" Soon muft our deftin'd courfe be run,
" The dead ride fwift,—hurrah! 'tis done,
 " The marriage bed is near."

High

High grated iron doors, in vain
Barr'd their way.—With loofened rein
  Whil'ft William urg'd the fteed,
He ftruck the bolts ;—they open flew,
A church yard drear appear'd in view ;
  Their path was o'er the dead.

As now, half veil'd by clouds, the moon
With feebler ray, o'er objects fhone,
  Where tomb-ftones faint appear,
A grave new dug arrefts the pair,
Cry'd, William, and embrac'd the fair,
  " Our marriage bed is here."

Scarce had he fpoke, when, dire to tell,
His flefh like touchwood from him fell,
  His eyes forfook his head.
A fkull, and naked bones alone,
Supply the place of William gone,
  'Twas Death that clafp'd the maid.

           Wild,

Wild, fnorting fire, the courfer rear'd,

As wrapp'd in fmoke he difappear'd,

    Poor Leonora fell;

The hideous fpe&tres hover round,

Deep groans fhe hears from under ground,

    And fiends afcend from hell.

They dance, and cry, in dreadful howl,

" She afks no mercy for her foul;

    " Her earthly courfe is done.

" When mortals, rafh and impious! dare

" Contend with God, and court defpair,

    " We claim them as our own."

" Yet," thus was heard, in milder ftrains,

    " Call on the Lord, while life remains,

        " Unite your heart to his;

    " When Man repents and is refign'd,

    " God loves to foothe his fuff'ring mind,

        " And grant him future blifs."

" Wc

" We claim as our's, who impious dare

" Contend with God, and court defpair ;"

  Again the fpeƈtres cry'd.

" Fate threats in vain, when man's refign'd,

" God loves to foothe the fuff'ring mind,"

  The gentler voice reply'd.

Leonora, e'er her fenfe was gone,

Thus faint exclaim'd,—" thy Will be done,

  " Lord, let thy anger ceafe."

Soft on the wind was born the pray'r ;

The fpeƈtres vanifh'd into air,

  And all was hufh'd in peace.

Now redd'ning tints the fkies adorn,

And ftreaks of gold, proclaim the morn ;

  The night is chas'd away.

The fun afcends, new warmth he gives,

New hope, new joy ; all nature lives,

  And hails the glorious day.

No

No more are dreadful phantoms near;
Love, and his fmiling train, appear;
    They cull each fweeteft flow'r,
To fcatter o'er the path of youth,
To deck the bridal bed, when Truth
    And Beauty own their pow'r.

Ah,—could your pow'r avert the blaft
Which threatens Blifs!—could paffion laft!
    Ye dear enchanters tell;
What purer joy could Heaven beftow,
Than when with fhar'd affection's glow,
    Our panting bofoms fwell?

Sweet fpirits! wave the airy wand,
Two faithful hearts your care demand;
    Lo! bounding o'er the plain,
Led by your charm, a youth returns;
With hope, his breaft impatient burns;
    Hope is not always vain.

                              Wake,

" Wake, Leonora!—wake to Love!

" For thee, his choiceft wreath he wove ;"

  Death vainly aim'd his Dart.

The Paft was all a dream ; fhe woke—

He lives ;—'twas William's felf who fpoke,

  And clafp'd her to his Heart.

Blake. in   Perry. sc

Farþu nv þars
þic hafi allan gramir.

Edda Sæmundar.

London Printed for W. Miller. Old Bond Street.

LENORE.

EIN

GEDICHT.

VON

GOTTFRIED AUGUST BÜRGER.

~~~~~~

Hafte, hafte, he lies in wait, he's at the door,
Infidious *Death!* fhould his ftrong hand arreft,
No compofition fets the prifoner free.
Eternity's inexorable chain
Faft binds; and vengeance claims the full arrear.

YOUNG.

~~~~~~~~~~

LONDON:
GEDRUCHT BEY S. GOSNELL.

~~~

1796.

L E N O R E.

~~~~~~

LENORE fuhr um's Morgenroth
Empor aus ſchweren Träumen:
" Biſt untreu, Wilhelm, oder todt?
Wie lange willſt du ſäumen?"
Er war mit König Friedrich's Macht
Gezogen in die Prager Schlacht,
Und hatte nicht geſchrieben:
Ob er geſund geblieben.

<div align="center">B</div>

<div align="right">Der</div>

Der König und die Kaiferinn,
Des langen Haders müde,
Erweichten ihren harten Sinn,
Und machten endlich Friede;
Und jedes Heer, mit Sing und Sang,
Mit Paukenfchlag und Kling und Klang,
Gefchmückt mit grünen Reifern,
Zog heim zu feinen Häufern.

Und überall all überall,
Auf Wegen und auf Stegen,
Zog Alt und Jung dem Jubelfchall
Der Kommenden entgegen.
Gottlob! rief Kind und Gattinn laut,
Willkommen! manche frohe Braut.
Ach! aber für Lenoren
War Grufs und Kufs verlohren.

Sie frug den zug wohl auf und ab,
Und frug nach allen Nahmen;
Doch keiner war, der Kundfchaft gab,
Von allen, fo da kamen.
Als nun das Heer vorüber war,
Zerraufte fie ihr Rabenhaar,
Und warf fich hin zur Erde,
Mit wüthiger Geberde.

Die

Die Mutter lief wohl hin zu ihr:—
„ Ach, daſs ſich Gott erbarme!
Du trautes Kind, was iſt mit dir ?”—
Und ſchloſs ſie in die Arme.—
„ O Mutter, Mutter! hin iſt hin!
Nun fahre Welt und alles hin !
Bey Gott iſt kein Erbarmen.
O weh, O weh, mir Armen!”—

„ Hilf Gott, hilf! Sieh uns gnädig an!
Kind, bet' ein Vaterunſer!
Was Gott thut, das iſt wolgethan.
Gott, Gott erbarmt ſich Unſer !”—
„ O Mutter, Mutter! Eitler Wahn!
Gott hat an mir nicht wohlgethan!
Was half, was half mein Beten ?
Nun iſt's nicht mehr vonnöthen.”—

„ Hilf Gott, hilf! wer den Vater kennt,
Der weiſs, er hilft den Kindern.
Das hochgelobte Sakrament
Wird deinen Jammer lindern.”—
„ O Mutter, Mutter! was mich brennt,
Das lindert mir kein Sakrament!
Kein Sakrament mag Leben
Den Todten wiedergeben.”—

„ Hör,

„ Hör, Kind! wie, wenn der falfche Mann,
Im fernen Ungerlande,
Sich feines Glaubens abgethan,
Zum neuen Ehebande?
Lafs fahren, Kind, fein Herz dahin!
Er hat es nimmermehr Gewinn!
Wann Seel' und Leib fich trennen,
Wird ihn fein Meineid brennen.''—

„ O Mutter, Mutter! hin ift hin!
Verlohren ift verlohren!
Der Tod, der Tod ift mein Gewinn!
O wär' ich nie gebohren!
Lifch aus, mein Licht, auf ewig aus!
Stirb hin, ftirb hin in Nacht und Graus,
Bey Gott ift kein Erbarmen,
O weh, O weh, mir Armen!''—

„ Hilf Gott, hilf! Geh nicht ins Gericht
Mit deinem armen Kinde!
Sie wiefs nicht, was die Zunge fpricht.
Behalt ihr nicht die Sünde!
Ach, Kind, vergifs dein irdifch Leid,
Und denk an Gott und Seligkeit!
So wird doch deiner Seelen
Der Bräutigam nicht fehlen.''—

„ O Mut-

,, O Mutter!—was ift Seligkeit?
O Mutter! Was ift Hölle?
Bey ihm, bey ihm ift Seligkeit,
Und ohne Wilhelm Hölle!—
Lifch aus, mein Licht, auf ewig aus!
Stirb hin, ftirb hin in Nacht und Graus!
Ohn' ihn mag ich auf Erden,
Mag dort nicht felig werden."—

So wüthete, Verzweifelung
Ihr in Gehirn und Adern.
Sie fuhr mit Gottes Fürfehung
Vermeffen fort zu hadern;
Zerfchlug den Bufen, und zerrang
Die Hand, bis Sonnenuntergang,
Bis auf am Himmelfbogen
Die goldnen Sterne zogen.

Und auffen, horch! ging's trap trap trap,
Als wie von Roffefhufen,
Und klirrend ftieg ein Reiter ab,
An des Geländers Stufen;
Und horch! und horch! den Pfortenring
Ganz lofe, leife, klinglingling!
Dann kamen durch die Pforte
Vernehmlich diefe Worte.

C   ,, Holla

„ Holla, Holla! Thu auf mein Kind!
Schläfst, Liebchen, oder wachst du?
Wie bist noch gegen mich gesinnt?
Und weinest oder lachst du?"—
„ Ach, Wilhelm, du?—So spät bey Nacht?—
Geweinet hab' ich und gewacht;
Ach, grosses Leid erlitten!
Wo kommst du hergeritten?"—

„ Wir satteln nur um Mitternacht.
Weit ritt ich her von Böhmen.
Ich habe spät mich aufgemacht,
Und will dich mit mir nehmen."—
„ Ach, Wilhelm, erst herein geschwind!
*Den Hagedorn, durchsaust der Wind,
Herein, in meinen Armen,
Herzliebster, zu erwarmen!"—

„ Lass sausen durch den Hagedorn,
Lass sausen, Kind, lass sausen!
Der Rappe scharrt; es klirrt der Sporn.
Ich darf allhier nicht hausen.
Komm, schürze, spring' und schwinge dich
Auf meinen Rappen hinter mich!
Muss heut noch hundert Meilen
Mit dir in's Brautbett' eilen.

„ Ach

* Through the sharp hawthorn blows the cold wind.
Shakespear's King Lear, Act iii. Scene 4.

„ Ach ! wollteſt hundert Meilen noch
Mich heut in's Brautbett' tragen ?
Und horch ! es brummt die Glocke noch,
Die elf ſchon angeſchlagen.''—
„ Sieh hin, ſieh her ! der Mond ſcheint hell.
Wir und die Todten reiten ſchnell.
Ich bringe dich, zur Wette,
Noch heut ins Hochzeitbette.''—

„ Sag an, wo iſt dein Kämmerlein ?
Wo ? Wie dein Hochzeitbettchen ?''—
„ Weit, weit von hier !—Still, kuhl und klein !—
Sechs Bretter und zwey Brettchen !''—
„ Hat's Raum für mich ?''—„ Für dich und mich !
Komm, ſchürze, ſpring' und ſchwinge dich !
Die Hochzeitgäſte hoffen ;
Die Kammer ſteht uns offen.''—

Schön Liebchen ſchürzte, ſprang und ſchwang
Sich auf das Roſs behende ;
Wohl um den trauten Reiter ſchlang
Sie ihre lilienhände ;
Und hurre hurre, hop hop hop !
Ging's fort in ſauſendem Galopp,
Daſs Roſs und Reiter ſchnoben,
Und Kies und Funken ſtoben.

Zur

Zur rechten und zur linken Hand,
Vorbey vor ihren Blicken,
Wie flogen Anger, Haid' und Land!
Wie donnerten die Brücken!
„ Graut Liebchen auch ?—Der Mond fcheint hell!
Hurrah! die Todten reiten fchnell!
Graut Liebchen auch vor Todten ?"—
„ Ach nein!—Doch lafs die Todten!"—

Was klang dort für Gefang und Klang?
Was flatterten die Raben?
Horch Glockenklang! horch Todtenfang:
„ Lafst uns den Leib begraben!"
Und näher zog ein Leichenzug,
Der Sarg und Todtenbaare trug.
Das Lied war zu vergleichen
Dem Unkenruf in Teichen.

„ Nach Mitternacht begrabt den Leib,
„ Mit Klang und Sang und Klage!
„ Jetzt führ' ich heim mein junges Weib.
„ Mit, mit zum Brautgelage!
„ Komm, Küfter, hier! Komm mit dem Chor,
„ Und gurgle mir das Brautlied vor!
„ Komm, Pfaff', und fprich den Segen,
„ Eh wir zu Bett' uns legen!"—

Still

Still Klang und Sang.—Die Baare schwand.—
Gehorsam seinem Rufen,
Kam's, hurre hurre! nachgerannt,
Hart hinter's Rappen Hufen.
Und immer weiter, hop hop hop!
Ging's fort in saufendem Galopp,
Daſs Roſs und Reiter schnoben,
Und Kies und Funken stoben.

Wie flogen rechts, wie flogen links,
Gebirge, Bäum' und Hecken!
Wie flogen links, und rechts, und links
Die Dörfer, Städt' und Flecken!—
„ Graut Liebchen auch?—Der Mond scheint hell!
Hurrah! die Todten reiten schnell!
Graut Liebchen auch vor Todten?"—
„ Ach! Laſs sie ruhn die Todten."—

Sieh da! sieh da! Am Hochgericht
Tanzt' um des Rades Spindel
Halb sichtbarlich bey Mondenlicht,
Ein luftiges Gesindel.—
Saſa! Gesindel, hier! Komm hier!
Gesindel, komm und folge mir!
Tanz' uns den Hochzeitreigen,
Wann wir zu Bette steigen!"—

D   **Und**

Und das Gefindel, hufch, hufch, hufch!
Kam hinten nachgepraffelt;
Wie Wirbelwind am Hafelbufch
Durch dürre Blätter raffelt.
Und weiter, weiter, hop hop hop!
Ging's fort in faufendem Galopp,
Dafs Rofs und Reiter fchnoben
Und Kies und Funken ftoben.

Wie flog, was rund der Mond befchien,
Wie flog es in die Ferne!
Wie flogen oben über hin
Der Himmel und die Sterne!—
Graut Liebchen auch ?—Der Mond fcheint hell!
Hurrah! die Todten reiten fchnell!
„ Graut Liebchen auch vor Todten ?"—
„ O weh! Lafs ruhn die Todten!"—

„ Rapp'! Rapp'! Mich dünkt der Hahn fchon ruft.
Bald wird der Sand verrinnen—
Rapp'! Rapp'! Ich wittre Morgenluft—
Rapp' Tummle dich von hinnen!—
Vollbracht, vollbracht ift unfer Lauf!
Das Hochzeitbette thut fich auf!
Die Todten reiten fchnelle!
Wir find, wir find zur Stelle."—

Rafch

Rasch auf ein eisern Gitterthor
Ging's mit verhängtem Zügel;
Mit schwanker Gert' ein Schlag davor,
Zersprengte Schloss und Riegel.
Die Flügel flogen klirrend auf,
Und über Grüber ging der Lauf.
Es blinkten Leichensteine
Rund um im Mondenscheine.

Ha sieh! ha sieh! im Augenblick,
Huhu! ein gräfslich Wunder!
Des Reiters Koller, Stück für Stück,
Fiel ab, wie muerber Zunder,
Zum Schädel, ohne Zopf und Schopf,
Zum nackten Schädel ward sein Kopf;
Sein Körper zum Gerippe,
Mit Stundenglas und Hippe.

Hoch bäumte sich, wild schnob der Rapp',
Und sprühte Feuerfunken;
Und hui! war's unter ihr hinab
Verschwunden und versunken.
Geheul! Geheul! aus hoher Luft,
Gewinsel kam aus tiefer Gruft.
Lenorens Herz, mit Beben,
Rang zwischen Tod und Leben.

Nun

Nun tanzten wohl bey Mondenglanz,
Rund um herum im Kreife,
Die Geifter einen Kettentanz,
Und heulten diefe Weife:
, Geduld! Geduld! Wenn's Herz auch bricht!
Mit Gott im Himmel hadre nicht!
Des Leibes bift du ledig;
Gott fey der Seele gnädig!"